MY FIRST LOOK AT SCIENCE

**HEAT FROM THE SUN HELPS PLANTS GROW**

# Temperature

MELISSA GISH

Published by Creative Education

123 South Broad Street, Mankato, Minnesota 56001

Creative Education is an imprint of The Creative Company

Designed by Rita Marshall

Photographs by Corbis (Matt Brown, George B. Diebold, George McCarthy, David Pollack), Getty

Images (Mitch Epstein, Romilly Lockyer, Lori Adamski Peek, David Waldorf), KAC Productions, Ted

Kinsman, Tom Stack and Associates

Cover illustration © 1996 Roberto Innocenti

Printed in the United States of America

**Library of Congress Cataloging-in-Publication Data**

Gish, Melissa. Temperature / by Melissa Gish.

p. cm. — (My first look at science)

Includes index.

ISBN 1-58341-375-8

1. Temperature—Juvenile literature. 2. Heat—Juvenile literature. 3. Molecules—Juvenile literature. I.

Title. II. Series.

QC256.G57 2005     536.5—dc22     2004055263

First edition  9 8 7 6 5 4 3 2 1

# Temperature

## MOVING MOLECULES

Everything in the world is made of tiny things called molecules. Your body is made of molecules. You cannot see them, but they are moving all the time.

Think of molecules as little marbles in a cup. If you put a few marbles in the cup, they will move around a lot when you shake the cup. But if you pack the cup with lots of marbles, they will not move much.

**MOLECULES MOVE AROUND LIKE MARBLES**

This movement is related to temperature. When molecules are packed loosely, they can move around quickly. Fast-moving molecules make things feel hot. Molecules that are packed tightly move slowly. Slow-moving molecules make things feel cold.

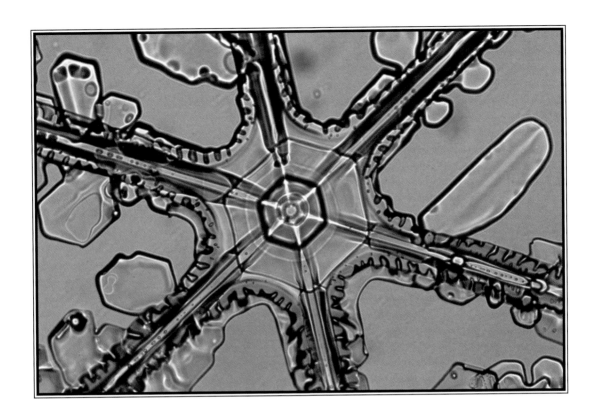

Things that are very

hot or cold are dangerous.

Fire or very cold water

can hurt you.

**SNOWSTORMS HAPPEN DURING COLD WINTERS**

# MEASURING TEMPERATURE

We can feel if something is cool or warm by touching it. But touch does not tell us exactly how cool or how warm it is. The temperature must be measured. We have two **scales** for measuring temperature. They are called Fahrenheit and Celsius.

Venus is a planet close

to the sun. It is very hot.

Pluto is a planet far away.

It is very cold.

We use a **thermometer** to check the temperature of something. Your body has a normal temperature of 98.6 degrees Fahrenheit (36.9 degrees Celsius). If you have a **fever**, a thermometer will show that your temperature is higher. This means the molecules in your body are moving around faster.

**A THERMOMETER SHOWS BODY TEMPERATURE**

## Bigger or Smaller

When things get hotter, they usually get bigger. A balloon left in the sunshine will get bigger. This is because the molecules inside bounce around quickly. They push hard against the inside of the balloon.

But if you put the balloon in the refrigerator, it will shrink. This is because the molecules slow down. They do not push as hard against the inside of the balloon.

Summer days are hot.

But the surface of the sun

is 100 times hotter than

the hottest day on Earth!

**BALLOONS GET BIGGER WHEN IT IS HOT**

Builders know that temperature makes things change size. This is why sidewalks are made with cracks between the sections. In the summer, sidewalks get hot. The cracks let the sidewalks **expand** without breaking.

## Everything Has Heat

Molecules are always moving, so every object in the world has some heat. Even an ice cube has some heat. Its molecules are moving slowly, but they are still moving.

**EVERYTHING HAS SOME HEAT—EVEN SNOWMEN**

There are even molecules in outer space. They move very slow, though. This makes outer space four times colder than the North Pole! Astronauts have to wear special suits to stay warm.

Sunlight and fire can make things warmer. Darkness and ice can make them colder. Everything has a temperature that can be measured. Rocks, water, shoes, and you!

Some animals sleep
through winter.
Their temperature gets
lower during this time.

A MOUSE SLEEPING IN ITS WINTER NEST

# Hands-on: Moving Molecules

You can see how molecules move with this experiment. Ask a grown-up to help you.

## What You Need

A bowl of cold water          Food coloring

A bowl of hot water

## What You Do

1. Let the bowls sit so the water is very still.
2. Put one drop of food coloring in the cold water. Watch what happens.
3. Put one drop of food coloring in the hot water. Watch what happens.

The cold water molecules are moving slowly. They make the coloring move around only a little. The hot water molecules are moving quickly. They make the coloring move around a lot more.

**THE MOLECULES IN WATER ARE ALWAYS MOVING**

## Index

## Words to Know

**expand**—to get bigger or spread out

**fever**—an increase in body temperature when a person is sick

**scales**—systems that have numbers and are used to measure something

**thermometer**—a special tube used to measure how hot or cold something is

## Read More

Gardner, Robert. *Really Hot Science Projects With Temperature: How Hot Is It? How Cold Is It?* Springfield, N.J.: Enslow, 2003.

Neil, Ardy. *The Science Book of Hot and Cold.* San Diego: Harcourt Brace Jovanovich, 1992.

Stille, Darlene R. *Hot and Cold.* Minneapolis: Compass Point Books, 2001.

## Explore the Web

**Energy Quest: Science Projects** http://www.energyquest.ca.gov/projects

**Temperature World** http://www.temperatureworld.com

**Who Invented the Thermometer?**

http://www.brannan.co.uk/thermometers/invention.html